Frau Wibrandis

Frau Wibrandis

A Woman in the Time of Reformation

Ernst Staehelin

*Translated with Introduction, Notes,
and Illustrations by
Ed. L. Miller, with Ingalisa Reicke*

WIPF & STOCK · Eugene, Oregon

FRAU WIBRANDIS
A Woman in the Time of Reformation

Copyright © 2009 Ed. L. Miller. All rights reserved. Except for brief quotations in critical publications or reviews, no part of this book may be reproduced in any manner without prior written permission from the publisher. Write: Permissions, Wipf and Stock Publishers, 199 W. 8th Ave., Suite 3, Eugene, OR 97401.

Wipf and Stock Publishers
199 W. 8th Ave., Suite 3
Eugene, OR 97401

www.wipfandstock.com

ISBN 13: 978-1-55635-508-0

English Translation Copyright © 2007, Ed. L. Miller. Originally published as *Frau Wibrandis: Eine Gestalt aus den Kämpfen der Reformationszeit,* Gotthelf-Verlag, Bern and Leipzig, 1934. All Rights Reserved.

Manufactured in the U.S.A.

Contents

Translator's Introduction / vii

1 Basel and Strasbourg / 1
2 Wibrandis' Origins / 10
3 With Oecolampadius in Basel / 15
4 With Capito in Strasbourg / 27
5 With Bucer in Strasbourg / 31
6 Years of Exile: England / 36
7 A Widow in Strasbourg and Basel / 48
8 Children and Grandchildren / 54

Picture Credits / 57

Bibliographical Note / 59

Translator's Introduction

MY INTEREST in this little-known sixteenth-century woman, Wibrandis (pronounced *Vibran'dis*) Rosenblatt, stems from my days as a doctoral student in theology at the University of Basel, Switzerland. I was preparing myself for an oral examination in which, among other things, I would be asked about Johannes Oecolampadius, the Reformer of Basel. I found my way immediately to the extensive work of Ernst Staehelin. Staehelin, who died in 1980, was at the time a retired professor of the theology faculty, a kindly yet imposing man with a great shock of white hair. He was always willing to chat with students in the coffee shop on the fourth floor of the university library. He was a sort of Grand Old Man of Basel, and he had written widely on the time of Reformation in Basel.

I dutifully took in what I could of Staehelin's various works on Oecolampadius, and, almost incidentally, his little book on Oecolampadius' wife, *Frau Wibrandis: Eine Gestalt aus den Kämpfen der Reformationszeit*. From the latter, my impression was immediate: Oecolampadius, to be sure, was an important and even decisive figure in the troubled days of the religious Reformation in Switzerland, and his role in the Reformation of Basel, in particular, can hardly be overstated.

But the real *person* in the story was his obscure wife. Hers is truly a poignant and personal story of loves and losses, hopes and hardships, as the briefest outline of her life reveals: She was married four times and widowed four times; she was the mother of children by all of them and the stepmother of many; she stood in the background, but at the same time as a real participant in the theological and political turmoil of the day; and she lived in the nightmare of two plague epidemics which claimed one of her husbands, several of her children, and finally herself. Amidst all of this, we encounter, as I have said, a *real person*, a *woman*. The evidence for the life of Wibrandis is fragmentary, and often we know her only as she is reflected by the males who dominate her story. Nonetheless, she emerges over all the centuries as yet recognizable by us.

There are several reasons for attending to this little story of Wibrandis. *First*, it provides a kind of review of the whole Reformation scene, important for anyone interested in the emergence of our modern western heritage. It was, truth to tell, incalculably determinative for who we are today. In the story of Wibrandis, we encounter the names (for example, of Oecolampadius, Capito, and Bucer), the central places (Basel, Zurich, and Strasbourg), some of the central events (the Second Kappel War, the Marburg Colloquy, and the troubled Basel days of February 1529), and some of the central issues (iconoclasm, religious tolerance, and the debate over the Lord's Supper).

Second, Wibrandis' story provides a glimpse into the work-a-day, domestic, familial life of those days. To be sure, what is displayed here is, more specifically, the daily life of the sixteenth-century Protestant parsonage. But that itself—the first generation of the Protestant parsonage—is a culturally interesting phenomenon, though in many respects such a home was similar to any other at the time.

Third, and turning to the still more personal and human interest of the story, many readers may find the letters (actually, fragments of letters) which are quoted along the way to be the most significant part of Staehelin's account. The letters were written in a variety of circumstances and with quite differing ends in view, but they usually provide glimpses into a soul. Oecolampadius' original letter to Zwingli displays something of the passion with which the Reformers understood their laborers for God; one will smile at the way Aletheia Oecolampadius addresses her husband as "my kind, dear master," without hesitating to give him a piece of her mind as to what he should say and do at the conference he is attending; many a mother will identify with Wibrandis who, in a letter to her wayward son, tells him, as it were, either to "straighten up" or not to expect any help from home; and then there is the almost unspeakable tenderness with which Bucer writes encouragingly (and with some discernible streaks of guilt) to his mentally deficient son. The letters, perhaps more than anything, put us in touch with those real people, trying to make their way and their contribution in a difficult time.

Finally, it is the story of a woman in a man's world, almost totally eclipsed by the illustrious men in her life. She bore the brunt of it.

For those who may find Staehelin's style sometimes quaint and sometimes overly pious, it must be remembered that the book was originally published in 1934, from a self-consciously Christian and Protestant perspective, and for a community, that, unlike ours, was knowledgeable about and proud of its religious heritage. I have added clarifying notes for some of the more important names, events, issues, and the like, and a map by which the reader can identify some of the more important places. I have also included pictures that may help to flesh-out the people and events depicted. A bibliographical note provides sources of citations and other such information. Of course, none of this collateral material is part of Staehelin's original book that didn't even have footnotes.

Staehelin, whose family descended from Wibrandis, named one of his daughters after her, and he dedicated his book "to my dear little daughter Wibrandis." This leads me to mention another woman of Basel, though a contemporary and of Swedish descent. Mrs. Ingalisa Reicke, who, along with her husband, Professor Bo Reicke (late New Testament scholar at the University of Basel), has provided untold support, spiritually and materially, for innumerable students, often Americans. A scholar in her own right (M.A., University of Uppsala), she has had a great interest in this present project, has carefully checked and improved the translation, and has otherwise contributed to the collateral material.

My thanks, further, to Dr. Amy Burnett of Nebraska State University, and to Dr. Paul Keyser of the Watson Research Center, both of whom had a hand in checking the translation, and to Mr. Erik Hanson, Mr. Lyle Mahon, and Ingrid Fischer for additional assistance.

Basel and Environs

I

Basel and Strasbourg

Zurich, Basel, and Strasbourg formed the great centers of the Reformation movement in the region of the upper Rhine.[1] The Reformers of these three cities formed a close alliance that fought the great battle of faith.

Johannes Oecolampadius

1. The Rhine River flows out of Lake Constance northward to Mainz; its headwaters lie in the Alps, whence it flows into the east end of Lake Constance.

The bond between the Zurich Reformer, Ulrich Zwingli,[2] and the Basel Reformer, Johannes Oecolampadius,[3] is well-known. No sooner had Oecolampadius arrived in November 1522 for his last sojourn in Basel before he turned to the bold leader in Zurich:

> Who could not regard as friend one who so zealously defends the things of Christ, who so faithfully tends his sheep, whom the wolves must greatly fear, who positions himself as a strong wall before the house of Israel, who, in word and deed, exemplifies to us the old men of faith. . . . Fight on and be victorious! I don't mean for your own sake, for that certainly isn't what you want. You know the passage: "Let each of you look not to your own

---

2. Ulrich Zwingli (1484–1531) was a native of Switzerland, educated at Bern, Basel, and Vienna, and was ordained to the Roman Catholic priesthood in 1506. Through the influence of the great Roman Catholic humanist, Erasmus, he became critical of church abuses. In 1518, he was appointed Minister in Zurich where he remained the rest of his life. Here he inaugurated ecclesiastical and political reforms, wrote many influential works, and led Zurich into the Reformed movement that was gaining momentum in Switzerland. He was killed in the Second Battle of Kappel (Reformers vs. Catholics) in 1531.

3. Johannes Oecolampadius (1482–1531), originally "Huszgen," which was refashioned into "Hausschein," "light of the house," and then Latinized into "Oecolampadius," hailed from Weinsberg, Germany. He was educated in Weinsberg, Heilbronn, and Heidelberg, and appointed Priest in Weinsberg. At one point he joined a monastery, but fled it because of his own increasingly Reformed ideas. He made several sojourns in Basel where he assisted Erasmus in producing the first printed edition of the New Greek Testament, and where he finally settled as a theology professor, pastor, and leader of the Reformation in that city.

interests, but to the interests of others."[4] So, be victorious for Christ.

Dear Zwingli, may our solidarity in Christ be established through this little letter.[5]

Thus, the two men found each other. From now on they fought together for the renewal of the church in the Swiss Federation, and together they grappled with Luther[6] over the interpretation of the Lord's Supper. In fact, even their callings from the earthly theater occurred in common: A few weeks after Zwingli's death on the battlefield of Kappel,[7] Oecolampadius

---

4. Phil. 2:4 (all scripture quotations are from the New Revised Standard Version).

5. Johannes Oecolampadius (1482–1531), originally "Huszgen," which was refashioned into "Hausschein," "light of the house," and then Latinized into "Oecolampadius," hailed from Weinsberg, Germany. He was educated in Weinsberg, Heilbronn, and Heidelberg, and appointed Priest in Weinsberg. At one point he joined a monastery, but fled it because of his own increasingly Reformed ideas. He made several sojourns in Basel where he assisted Erasmus in producing the first printed edition of the New Greek Testament, and where he finally settled as a theology professor, pastor, and leader of the Reformation in that city.

6. Martin Luther (1483–1546) was the leading figure of the Reformation. Originally a monk, he challenged church abuses such as the sale of "indulgences" through which individuals could purchase partial remission of punishment for sin, and advocated a stark doctrine of justification by faith alone. He authored numerous commentaries on Biblical books and also theological treatises, but, most importantly, translated the Bible into the German vernacular. The nailing of his "Ninety-five Theses" (against the Roman Catholic Church) on the door of the Castle Church in Wittenburg on October 31, 1517, is usually regarded as the symbolic origin of the Protestant Reformation. Many of his works were published in Basel.

7. In June 1529, a military force from Reformed Zurich met a Catholic force at Kappel, south of Zurich. War was averted and an armistice was declared, called the First Peace of Kappel. Zwingli, however, subsequently

Ulrich Zwingli

also died. The cause was blood poisoning occasioned by an abscess, though his shock over the catastrophe of the Kappel War must have also left its mark.

No less important was Oecolampadius' relation to the Reformers of Strasbourg: Matthäus Zell, Wolfgang Fabricius Capito, Martin Bucer, and Kaspar Hedio. Especially with Capito[8] and Bucer,[9] he formed a close circle of friendship as well as a partnership of thought and work.

The relationship between Oecolampadius and Capito was established about 1514: Oecolampadius was studying Greek and Hebrew in Heidelberg while Capito held the office of Preacher in Bruchsal. From that time they were closely associated. In January 1522, Oecolampadius fled the Alto Münster monas-

---

established an effective blockade of the five (Catholic) "forest" Cantons, setting off a second confrontation at Kappel in October, 1531. The Reformed forces were decisively beaten and the Second Peace of Kappel was enacted, insuring coexistence of the Reformed and Catholic Cantons.

8. Wolfgang Fabricius Capito (1478–1541) was trained in law and theology in Freiburg, Germany. He was a preacher and professor in Basel (where he was associated with the humanist work of Erasmus), then a preacher and advisor to the Archbishop in Mainz. He came to Strasbourg as Professor and Preacher in 1523, and inaugurated the Reformation of that city, advocating nonviolent and tolerant methods of reform.

9. Martin Bucer (1491–1551), whose name was Latinized from Butzer, was born and raised in Selestat, a few miles south of Strasbourg. In 1506, he entered the Dominican Order, but fell under the spell of Luther, left the monastery, married, and was excommunicated. He became inclined (against Luther) to the Zwinglian view of the Eucharist, and, after Zwingli's death, was the leader of the Reformation, not only in Strasbourg, but in the whole region. Due to a political-ecclesiastical reversal, in 1549 (as we shall see) he was forced into exile in England, where he was embraced by Edward V and Thomas Cranmer, was made Professor of Divinity at Cambridge, and died soon after.

tery[10] to escape silencing by his adversaries and went into hiding temporarily; Capito arranged with his master, the Archbishop of Mainz and Madgeburg, for an immediate leave, and rushed from Halle in an exhausting ride south to search out and possibly rescue his friend from the plottings of his enemies. The way led him also to Mainz, and to Kasper Hedio who, at the time, was Cathedral Preacher there. What a surprise and pleasure it was when Capito found the refugee in congenial conversation with Hedio! Soon all three were working in the two allied sister cities on the upper Rhine: Oecolampadius became Professor in Basel, and, at the same time, Pastor at St. Martin's Church and later at the Cathedral[11]; Capito moved to Strasbourg as Provost of St. Thomas' *Stift*,[12] and soon also took over the office of Preacher at New St. Peter's, as well as Theological Lecturer. In a copious exchange of letters, they supported one another in their struggles and troubles. And when Oecolampadius died, Capito took it on himself to finish and publish Oecolampadius' uncompleted commentaries on the Prophets Jeremiah and Ezekiel.

Oecolampadius' connection with Martin Bucer began when the latter came to Strasbourg as a refugee preacher, and, in 1524, became Pastor at St. Aurelien's. An increasingly close working relationship developed. Together they struggled for the independence of the church over against the state, for the introduction of the Office of Elders of the Church, and for the maintenance of discipline within the church. Together, they sought

10. The Monastery of St. Bridget in Alto Munster, near Augsburg.

11. At this time, the Cathedral Church in Basel was a Cathedral in the proper sense (the Church in which the Bishop presided), though after the Reformation it was, of course, a Cathedral in name only (in German, *Das Münster*).

12. A home for students of theology, still existing. Among its leaders in the last century was the celebrated Albert Schweitzer and the New Testament theologian, Oscar Cullmann.

to prevent the split of Protestantism into a Lutheran faction and a Reformed faction.[13] Together, they laid the foundation for the reorganization of the Waldensian Church.[14] Together, in the summer of 1531, along with Ambrosius Blarer of Constance,[15] they carried out the Reformation of the city and region of Ulm. Soon after Oecolampadius died, Bucer wrote to Blarer:

> You are rightly shaken by Oecolampadius' passing. We had no greater theologian than him, and his whole concern was the formation of a pure Church.

Hand in hand with these connections between Strasbourg and Basel, there are others.

The City Chancellor of Basel, Kasper Schaller, a leading personality in Basel at that time, hailed from Strasbourg and maintained important connections with the men of influence in his hometown. He visited there often to discuss and settle common concerns.

A connection between Basel and Strasbourg was also established through Konrad Hubert from Bergzabern. As a youth he was Oecolampadius' secretary, and for many years, on Ember

---

13. As it developed, the "Reformed" branch of the Reformation had its roots primarily in the teachings of Calvin (in contrast to those of Luther), though originally also in the teachings of Zwingli, Bucer, and others south and west of the Rhine.

14. The Waldensians, often seen as forerunners of the Reformation, arose at the end of the twelfth century in southern France under the leadership of Pierre Waldo, and allied themselves with the Reformation in the sixteenth century.

15. Ambrosius Blarer (1492–1564) was a Benedictine monk who fell under the influence of Luther and Melanchthon, left the monastery in 1522, and was active for the evangelical faith in Constance, Württemberg, and Switzerland.

Ambrosius Blarer

Day,[16] he fetched Oecolampadius' professor's pay at the city treasury. In 1529, Oecolampadius released him so he could be a proper student, but then on the occasion of his trip to Ulm took him along once more. There, Bucer met him and persuaded him to become his own assistant at St. Thomas' in Strasbourg, and also immediately produced for him a godly wife from Constance. Pastor Konrad and his wife, Margaretha, would be pillars of Reformed Strasbourg well into the second half of the sixteenth century.

In this partnership of struggle and labor on behalf of the church of Jesus Christ linking Basel and Strasbourg, stood the remarkable Wibrandis Rosenblatt.

---

16. Any day in the three-day period of prayer and fasting observed quarterly (Wednesday, Friday, and Saturday, following the first Sundays after Lent, Whitsunday, September 14, and December 13) by the Roman Catholic Church and other western churches.

2

Wibrandis' Origins

IN THE Dinkelberg,[1] the charming range of hills which rises between the Rhine and its tributary, the Wiese, east of Basel, there were in the middle ages two pilgrimage sites: One called Chrischona and the other, about two hours east of Chrischona, in Eichsel.[2] In Chrischona, the grave of the Holy Chrischona (Christiana) was venerated, while in Eichsel the object of the pilgrimage was the graves of three holy virgins. Since the thirteenth-century there is evidence for the beautiful German names: Kunegundis, Mechtundis, and Wibrandis. The name "Wibrandis," which interests us here, appears to mean "battle sword," from the combination of the two stems *viga* (= battle) and *branda* (= sword). It's hard to say whether any historicity attaches to the three virgins of Eichsel, whether their cult developed out of an ancient pagan veneration of three female deities, or whether some other origin should be considered. In any case, the report that they had belonged to the eleven thousand virgins who set out with St. Ursula for Rome is, along with the whole story of St. Ursula, the stuff of legends.[3]

At the end of the middle ages, the pilgrimages to the sacred sites of the Dinkelberg declined. Then, in the year 1504, while the papal legate, Cardinal Raymundus Peraudi, was in Basel,

1. "Dinkel"(= spelt) often is used in geographical names for a variety of wheat (*triticum*) cultivated in central-europe in the old days.

2. That is, by foot or wagon; today about fifteen minutes by car.

3. In the legend's fully developed form, a British princess, later canonized as St. Ursula, led eleven thousand virgins on a pilgrimage to Rome, and, on their return, were massacred at Cologne by the Huns.

the clergy and laymen of the region seized the opportunity to petition this exalted church dignitary to establish the sanctity of the four virgins of Chrischona and Eichsel; the bones would be elevated to the altar,[4] and both pilgrimages endowed with new life. The Cardinal had determined that some eminent Basel theologians should immediately and thoroughly investigate the matter. Many witnesses were presented and numerous miracles were authenticated, including traditional and, more important, recent accounts. On the basis of the investigation, the Cardinal performed the solemn Elevation of the Bones on June 16 in Eichsel and on June 17 in Chrischona, in the presence of the Bishop of Basel, Christoph von Utenheim, and other princes of the church, and amidst the participation of a great crowd.

In the same year, 1504, when the names of the four saints—Chrischona, Kunegundis, Mechtundis, and Wibrandis—were on everyone's lips, a daughter was born to Hans Rosenblatt (from the nearby town of Säckingen) and to his wife Magdalena Strub (from Basel). She was named "Wibrandis."

According to family tradition, the Rosenblatts, then of the Hapsburg dominated town of Säckingen, descended from Swedish nobility. Such a descent, however, is more than doubtful. It's much more probable that the family was good Alemannic[5] stock, and got its name from a residence called *Zum Rosenblatt*,[6] just as similar names were common at that time in Switzerland, for example, "Rosenbaum," "Rosenburg," and "Rosenstock."

Of the father, Hans Rosenblatt, we know very little. In the year 1510, he is certainly identified as Mayor of Säckingen

4. The Elevation of the Bones to the altar as objects of veneration was, and is, the final stage in the process of canonization.

5. Alemannia: a confederation of German tribes which, dating from as early as the third century, settled areas of Alsace, southwestern Germany, and Switzerland.

6. Literally, "To the Rose Petal."

Wibrandis Rosenblatt

and he might have occupied this office for some time. In 1504, when Wibrandis was born, he was said to have fought in the war of Bavarian succession on the side of his sovereign, Emperor Maximilian, specifically in the bloody battle of Regensburg, and in the conquest of the powerful fortress of Kufstein. For his bravery he was knighted by the Emperor. Wibrandis' mother descended from the Basel family, Strub. This family operated a tannery, and several family members sat on the City Council as representatives of the Tanners' Guild. Magdalena appears to have spent her youth in the house *Zum Kienberg* on Barfüsserplatz.[7]

Besides the daughter Wibrandis, Magdalena presented her husband with a son, Adelberg Rosenblatt. We meet him later as a Journeyman Minter in Basel and Master Minter in Colmar.

The father, Hans Rosenblatt, appears often to have gallivanted hither and yon in imperial service far from home, with the result that the mother, with her children Wibrandis and Adelberg, moved to her native town of Basel. In 1521, Emperor Karl V allotted to him a lordly estate in Austria as recompense for the soldier's pay owed him. His wife, nevertheless, preferred the position of a lady of the Republic of Basel[8] to that of a mistress of an Austrian castle.

In 1524, Wibrandis Rosenblatt married the distinguished Master of Liberal Arts, Ludwig Keller, the son of the clothier, Clemens Keller. The marriage produced a daughter who received the mother's name: Wibrandis. But, already in the summer of

7. A center of activity in both old and contemporary Basel, so-named from the monastery of barefooted Franciscans (*Barfüsser*). The buildings of the convent have disappeared, but the church (now a historical museum) still stands and dominates the square.

8. Basel joined the Swiss Confederation in 1501 as a republic governed by Guilds, or associations, geared to the promotion of various trades. The office of Masters of the Guilds was, in some families, inherited. Wibrandis Rosenblatt belonged to such an association through her mother.

1526, Ludwig Keller was snatched away by death, leaving his young wife a widow.

3

With Oecolampadius in Basel

According to the Protestant understanding, celibacy is not a more exalted state. The essential point in God's eyes is that, whether married or not, we live in his power and purity and are ready to serve him with all we have. For this reason, the Reformers abandoned the demand of priestly celibacy, and created the Protestant parsonage as a new way of serving the community of Jesus Christ. Accordingly, Luther established his household with Katharina von Bora, Zwingli with Anna Reinhard, Bucer with Elizabeth Silbereisen, Capito with Agnes Röttel, Matthäus Zell with the especially distinguished Katharina Schütz. Likewise, some Basel pastors married.

Already in February of 1524, in a public Disputation,[1] Oecolampadius had also come out for the marriage of pastors. He himself, however, remained for the moment unmarried. An elderly housekeeper did the housework for him in the parsonage at St. Martin's, and attended also to the boarders who were entrusted to the learned pastor and professor, such as the son of the famous Konrad Peutinger, town clerk of Augsburg, or the sons of Jakob Kirser, the Chancellor of Baden.

In January of 1527, Oecolampadius for the first time took a step towards marriage. How important this step was, not only for Oecolampadius, but also for the whole Basel Reformation movement, is apparent: he discussed the matter with the chief Guild Master, Jakob Meyer of Hirzen (who later became the

1. Disputations, in which theses were formally debated, were at the time a standard and popular way of addressing theological issues, and were sponsored frequently by both Catholics and Protestants.

Mayor of Basel and the spiritual leader of the Reformation in the town hall), and also with the Reformers of Zurich and Strasbourg. Capito wrote to him: Marriage is an honorable and holy state, especially for a Christian and pastor. Oecolampadius replied that the heavenly Father governs our affairs; yet, he was at liberty, he can either marry a Christian sister or remain single. Perhaps he had thought already of Frau Wibrandis. In any case, he mentioned a widow of respectable reputation who was, in Christ, devotedly attached to him.

Nevertheless, for the moment the whole thing died down, and Oecolampadius' elderly parents moved from Weinsberg into the parsonage at St. Martin's in Basel—his father, Johannes Hausschein, and his mother Anna Pfister, a native of Basel. Supervision of the household was immediately taken on by his mother.

But, five days after Oecolampadius returned from the Disputation at Bern, at the beginning of February 1528, she died. He reported to Zwingli that the burden of household cares would now fall to him more heavily than before, probably because, in addition, his elderly father had to be cared for. And so, with extreme haste, he decided now to carry out what he had seriously considered one year earlier: In March of 1528, he contracted the covenant of marriage with Frau Wibrandis. Oecolampadius wrote to Zwingli: "Pray to the Lord, that it may be blessed and redound to his glory"; the woman has many prominent foes as well as friends of the Gospel in her family; her dowry is small, but he wouldn't want it any larger. To Wilhelm

Desiderius Erasmus

Farel,[2] who at the time worked as a Reformer in Aigle,[3] he reported that God had given him a wife, a woman of Christian inclination, of modest means, but of respectable family, and having borne the cross for several years. To be sure, he would prefer her to be a few years older, but she displays no youthful immaturity. And, in another letter to Farel, he reports:

> She is quite well-versed in the knowledge of Christ, and she oversees the household with prudence. I couldn't wish it better.

It was to be expected, however, that this marriage of the 46-year-old Reformer with Wibrandis would be much ridiculed. In particular, a few not exactly complimentary comments were noted by the two literary scholars, Desiderius Erasmus and Bonifacius Amerbach.[4] On the other hand, friends near and far

---

2. William Farel (1489–1565) was, from the beginning, a leader of the French Reformation. He broke from Roman Catholicism in 1523 and took refuge in Basel. He was responsible for the spread of the "New Gospel" throughout French speaking Switzerland and beyond. With Pierre Viret, he accomplished the Reformation of Geneva, which, eventually, he turned over to the younger John Calvin, with whose name the "Reformed" branch of Protestantism was destined to become most associated.

3. A town in the Rhone Valley, east of Geneva, at that time dominated by the powerful city of Bern.

4. Desiderius Erasmus (1466?–1536), a Dutch scholar who, through his writings, did much to stimulate Christian interest in humanistic learning, including pagan Greek and Roman authors. As a Catholic, he addressed and opposed Luther, though reluctantly. He spent some of his most productive years in Basel, where, in 1516, he produced the first printed edition of the Greek New Testament, certainly one of the most important of his achievements. He is buried in the Basel Münster where a memorial may be viewed. Bonifacius Amerbach (1495–1562), a member of a distinguished Basel family, a Professor of Roman Law at the University, and a collector of fine art. A man of conciliatory nature, he

supported the marriage and commended it to the gracious governance of God. In this way, Wibrandis became linked through her husband's friendship with the Reformers' households in Zurich and Strasbourg. Greetings would be exchanged with Anna Reinhard, Agnes Röttel, and Elisabeth Silbereisen; Agnes Röttel would present Frau Wibrandis with a prayerbook—probably it was the *Little Biblical Prayerbook of the Fathers and Noble Women of the Old and New Testaments,* published by the Strasbourg schoolmaster, Otto Brunfels. In addition, physical well-being was not neglected; we learn from Frau Wibrandis that she provided the Swiss cheese for the Bucer household. She appears also to have been esteemed by the students; one of them, for example, sends his warm greetings to Oecolampadius and his "dear wife."

Amidst the final struggles for the success of the Reformation, the Guilds held large assemblies and in the middle of the night presented their demands to the City Council, and couriers departed from Basel for Zurich and Bern, and high-ranking emissaries from these cities rode off to Basel. On December 24, 1528, a son was born to Oecolampadius. He was named "Eusebius" (meaning "pious"). Distinguished godparents stood as sponsors at the baptism, among them one of the leading city elders of the Protestant faction, Johannes Irmi, and the wife of

---

pursued a middle course between that of the commentator and the critic. As a man on whom practical, rather than intellectual matters laid claim, he was a reorganizer and leader of the University, legal consultant to the city council, etc. The "unfriendly pronouncements" are worth reporting. Erasmus: "A few days ago Oecolampadius married a not inelegant girl with intent to castigate his flesh during Lent." Amerbach: "A decrepit old man with trembling head and body, so emaciated and wasted that you might well call him a living corpse, has married an elegant and blooming girl of 20, more or less." (Quoted in Roland Bainton, "Wibrandis Rosenblatt," in *Women of the Reformation in Germany and Italy* [Minneapolis: Augsburg, 1971], p. 81)

the aforementioned Guild Master and later Mayor, Jakob Meyer of Hirzen. The health of the little child was, initially, not good. In Oecolampadius' letter to his friend Capito, in which he reports the final breakthrough of the Basel Reformation and the iconoclastic riot of February 9, 1529,[5] he writes also that one must reckon with the child's possible death. Nevertheless, soon he was able to send a more optimistic report. Capito responds with delight, "Live well with your wife and precious offspring." And, on January 3, 1530, the record of the Gardeners' Guild announces with pride that "Dr. Johannes Hausschein, known as Oecolampadius, and Eusebius Hausschein, his son," had been admitted to membership. Also inducted into the Guild at this time were Albrecht Rosenblatt, who was a cousin of Frau Wibrandis, and Hieronymous Bothanus, Oecolampadius' assistant at St. Alban's.

Following the triumph of the Reformation, Oecolampadius moved to the position of Pastor of the Cathedral, and now, with his family, occupied the parsonage on Hasengässlein in the area of the present-day *Realgymnasium*.[6]

At the beginning of September 1529, an important visitor appeared at the door. It was Zwingli. He had secretly left Zurich in order to travel along with Oecolampadius to Marburg for a

5. On this date, swarms of Reformed-minded citizens, frustrated by the sluggish city council, overran the Cathedral for the purpose of destroying the "idolatrous" images that were, and are, so much a part of Roman Catholic worship. Precious statues were destroyed, paintings sliced up, stained glass windows shattered, statues dashed to the floor, and the central crucifix pulled down and dragged through the streets. To the present day, the vacant spot on the pedestal between the doors by the western portal where a statue of the Virgin once stood, testifies to the violence of this iconoclastic riot.

6. This secondary school, stressing modern languages has now moved elsewhere, but its nineteeth century building still stands where the Hasenglässlein once was.

Wolfgang Capito

conference with Luther on the Lord's Supper. The two Reformers were conveyed to Strasbourg by merchant ship, remained there a few days (they stayed with Matthäus and Katharina Zell), traveled by horse under military guard with the Strasbourgers, Bucer and Hedio, and after six weeks of excited discussion with Luther and his companions, and many hardships, they returned safe and sound. Upon their entry to Basel they were escorted by a squad of twenty riders. Zwingli remained in Basel for the next Sunday, preached in the Cathedral, and rode on to Zurich the next day.

One year later, Capito arrived from Strasbourg to travel with Oecolampadius to a conference in Zurich. Both coming and going, he was entertained royally by city and Guild chiefs at the *Gasthaus zum Storchen*. Soon after, Bucer arrived at the parsonage on Hasengässlein on his return trip from the Augsburger Reichstag and related his visit with Luther at Coburg. At the same time, two representatives of the Waldensians dropped in and held taxing discussions with the Basel Reformer; or the young Spaniard, Michael Servetus,[7] would turn up and beleaguer the busy pastor, professor, and church leader, in lengthy and tenacious argument. Such was the coming and going in the house of Frau Wibrandis. The pastors who had been dismissed because of their beliefs were especially numerous.

In the meantime, on March 21, 1530, a second child was born. It was a girl and was named "Irene" ("peace"). Her godparents included Simon Albrecht (Master of the Saffron Guild), and a lady from the family of Jakob von Rotberg (a country squire).

The spring and summer of 1531 brought especially difficult struggles when Oecolampadius sought to enforce church

---

7. A physician, whose Biblical studies led eventually to his heretical denial of the Trinity and the deity of Christ. He was finally arrested by Calvin, and, refusing to recant, was burned as a heretic in 1553.

Signatories to the agreements reached at the Marburg Colloquy, which did not include, however, agreement on the interpretation of the Lord's Supper

discipline: He helped put down the Anabaptist movement,[8] and in several sermons pointedly attacked the city council's administration of church property. It might happen, day or night and in his own home, that he would be confronted by his opponents in the most intense scenes; small uproars would break out when he visited the churches in the Basel region, or he might be summoned by the Council to defend his sermons. No doubt, Frau Wibrandis shared these trials and troubles with a concerned, steadfast, and also comforting spirit. Reluctantly, from May until July, 1531, and amidst these strains, Oecolampadius undertook a long trip to Ulm with its dangers and strains on body, soul, and spirit. When he returned, a third child had arrived, the daughter Aletheia ("truth"). Among her godparents, we find the City Chancellor, Heinrich Ryhiner, and the wife of Dr. Paul Phrygio, Pastor at St. Peter's and Professor of Theology. From the wife of the Ulm Reformer, Konrad Sam, Oeclampadius brought a gift for Wibrandis, the new mother.

In the autumn, the family was able to celebrate a pleasant little holiday. Already, in 1528, the parents had purchased a vineyard outside the city's Steinentor[9] in the direction of Binningen, and, in August 1531, they acquired a second vineyard, along with a meadow outside St. Alban's Gate. In September, there was always a jovial "gathering of the grapes." Johannes Gast, Oecolampadius' assistant at St. Martin's, appears also to have taken part.

8. The Anabaptists (literally, "rebaptizers") were a variety of groups, originating in the sixteenth century, who repudiated the practice of infant baptism and advocated "believers (or adult) baptism." They were denounced by the major Reformation leaders and sorely persecuted, often executed by drowning.

9. Basel was a fortified, or walled, city with five towered gates under guard, housing the main entrances. Still standing and restored are St. Alban's Gate, the Spalen Gate, and St. John's Gate.

Then, hard blows.

At the beginning of October, the Second Kappel War[10] broke out and Zwingli died on the battlefield. In a second battle, the men of Basel also suffered defeat in which Oecolampadius' assistant at St. Alban's, Hieronymous Bothanus, was killed.

Soon after, Oecolampadius himself became ill with an incurable ulcer, and, though the physicians summoned all their skills, the ulcer reached its critical point in the fourteen day struggle. On one of the last evenings, along with his wife and the rest of the family, he took communion, allowed the children to be brought to him, and said to Wibrandis and her mother, Magdalena Strub, "Take care that they become what is suggested by their names: pious, peace-loving, and truthful." In the early morning of November 23, he passed away. His burial in the cloisters[11] was attended by the entire

---

10. See Chapter 1, note 6.

11. The courtyard, bordered by covered walkways, adjacent to the Basel Münster. Here one can read yet today the epitaph mounted in 1532:

> D. IO: OECOLAPADIVS
> PROFESSIONE THEOLOGVS
> TRIVM LINGVARM
> PERTISSIMVS, AVTHOR
> EVANGELICAE DOCTRINAE
> IN HAC VRBE PRIMVS, ET TEMPLI HVIVS
> VERVS EPVS. VT
> DOCTRINA SIC VITAE
> SANCTIMONIA POLLENTISIMVS,
> SVB BREVE SAXV HOC.
> RECODITVS IACET.

("Concealed beneath this narrow slab lies Dr. Joh. Oecolampadius: theologian by profession, expert in three languages, first teacher of evangelical doctrine in this city, true overseer of this church, as in teaching so also very mighty in sanctity of life.")

city. The eulogy was delivered by old Telamonius Limpberger. On December 23, Wibrandis, "the widow of the very learned Johannes Oecolampadius," received the customary guardianship in the person of her uncle, the tanner, Martin Strub, while the children, Eusebius, Irene, and Aletheia, were made wards of the Councilman and butcher, Leonhard Pfister, a brother or nephew of Oecolampadius' mother.

4

With Capito in Strasbourg

WHILE OECOLAMPADIUS still lay on his sickbed, the report traveled from Strasbourg that Capito's wife, Agnes Röttel, had died. The Basel Professor, Simon Grynaeus, wrote to Bucer:

> You can't believe with what emotion Oecolampadius and I, along with my whole family, have learned of the death of Capito's wife. She was very close to us. But, since we don't want to be unthankful judges of God's blessings, we must consider it a great blessing to fall asleep in the Lord amidst all these traumatic events.

Capito, with his impracticality and inclination to depression, was especially hard hit by the passing of his wife. At a time when hasty marriage of the widowed was fully accepted, his friends soon began to coax him into a new marriage. Capito proposed first the widow of an Augsburg Anabaptist, and Bucer proposed the sister of Ambrosius Blarer in Constance. But, finally, it became evident to everyone (Martin Bucer, Ambrosius Blarer, Mayor Jakob Meyer, and especially Capito himself) that a union with Frau Wibrandis would be the happiest solution. In January 1532, Bucer wrote to Blarer that such a marriage would be wholly honorable and godly inasmuch as both the orphans of "so great a herald of Christ" would be cared for;[1] moreover, Frau Wibrandis was of a calm, discreet, and self-sacrificing spirit, and, therefore, would be of the greatest service. Thus, in April

---

1. Presumably an allusion to James 1:27.

1532, Capito and Frau Wibrandis were united, and she settled in as wife of the pastor of New St. Peter's in Strasbourg along with her children and mother, Magdalena Strub.

The life of the Strasbourg church was, at the time, especially rich and exciting. This was because of inner developments and debates, due to its leading role in the tasks, struggles, and troubles of Protestantism. Internally, a comprehensive "church polity" was implemented; as in Basel, there was a striving for the introduction of discipline within the church; and the Baptists, and all sorts of radicals, were continually stirring up trouble. In their relations to Protestantism in general, the question of the Lord's Supper stood foremost; the continuing efforts of the Strasbourgers, southern Germans, and Swiss to achieve harmony with the Lutherans is evident. Bucer was especially zealous in travels and consultations, but Capito did his fair share, too. The efforts were, nevertheless, only half-successful: The southern Germans, but not the Swiss, found themselves in agreement with the Lutherans. Along with these extraordinary pastoral duties went the usual ones of preparing sermons and lectures, and theological works had to be written as well. In such lively circumstances stood Frau Wibrandis, the wife of Capito, pastor's wife at New St. Peter's.

Then, too, there were domestic joys and suffering, numerous illnesses of the husband, financial troubles because of loans made to others by the good-hearted pastor, and, above all, the coming and going of children. In 1533, a daughter, Agnes, was born, and, following her in the next years, Dorothea, Johann Simon, Wolfgang Christoph, and Irene. Among the godparents of these children we encounter illustrious figures such as Martin Bucer, Katharina Zell, the great teacher Johann Sturm, and the Basel Professor, Simon Grynaeus. On the other hand, the little Irene Oecolampadius was already taken by death, and, in

Church of St. Thomas, Strasbourg

1541, the young Wibrandis Keller married a brass-worker from Strasbourg, Hans Jeliger.

Then, a horrendous plague came. The Basel historian Christian Wurstisen[2] reported:

> In the summer of 1541, there arose along the Rhine River, and in other places, a plague epidemic. Such an epidemic had already occurred a year before, but this one was somewhat worse, with the result that many were taken. At Strasbourg, 3,200 people died, not less at Colmar, 700 at Rheinfelden, and a considerable number at Basel. Noted persons who perished there included Jacob Meyer, Mayor, who, in this position had been an admirable instrument for the work of the Gospel; likewise, on the first day of August, Simon Grynaeus, a philosopher and theologian as well as Rector of the University. . . . On Christmas Eve, Dr. Andreas Bodenstein of Carolstadt died, Pastor at St. Peter's.

In Strasbourg, too, the evangelical parsonages were struck, and especially hard. In Hedio's house five children died. Bucer lost his wife, and, having already lost some of his ten children, now lost more, so that all that was left to him was his mentally and physically handicapped son, Nathaniel. And, in Capito's house, the children Eusebius Oecolampadius, Dorothea Wolfgang Christoph Capito, but, above all, Capito himself, were taken. Thus, Bucer lost his old comrade, and Frau Wibrandis (with her children, Aletheia Oecolampadius, Agnes, Johann Simon, and Irene Capito) was once again alone.

---

2. Christian Wurstisen (1544–1588), Professor of Theology and City Clerk, published his *Basler Chronik* in 1580, an important source for our knowledge of sixteenth-century Basel.

5

With Bucer in Strasbourg

CAPITO DIED one day before Bucer's wife. As she lay dying, she learned, from Katherine Zell, of Capito's death, and at dusk, summoning Frau Wibrandis, implored the widow to take her place (Frau Capito's) in Bucer's home. Likewise, she fervently begged her husband that after her death he would take Wibrandis as a new life partner. Bucer related to Ambrosius Blarer: "With tears I listened to her, but answered nothing."

Martin Bucer

Initially, Bucer's household was managed by Margarethe Hubert, but, with time, it became impossible to demand this of her. So, the wish of his deceased wife was about to be fulfilled. In March 1542, he wrote about it to Blarer:

> Pray to the Lord that what we intend may be accepted by Christ and be beneficial for the church. . . . God willing, after Easter we won't wait long to take the step. Don't talk about the matter beforehand, but wrestle with it in prayer (you and Johann Zwick and your brother), that the Lord may bring to pass what we have undertaken for his honor and for the progress of the church.

In fact, the wedding of Bucer and Wibrandis took place on April 16. In July, Bucer wrote again to Blarer:

> It's surely the Lord who has provided this helper in my cares and work. He provides so that I may obey and serve him, just as she, without a doubt, will serve me with faithfulness and devotion.

In 1529, Bucer exchanged the parsonage at St. Aurelien's for that of St. Thomas', and, accordingly, Wibrandis had now become the pastor's wife at St. Thomas'. Her children (Aletheia, Agnes, Johann Simon, and Irene), along with Nathaniel Bucer, filled that parsonage with new life. She was accompanied also by her mother, Magdalena Strub. Also belonging to the household, at least for a time, was Bucer's father and his second wife. Then there were the numerous guests who were happily accommodated.

How it went after Wibrandis' entrance into the Bucer parsonage is known from the report of a religious refugee from Italy, the former monk and priest, Peter Martyr Vermigli.[1] Via

---

1. Peter Martyr Vermigli (1500–1562) was born in Florence and

Zurich, he arrived in Basel with three companions. In Basel, the four Italians were hospitably put up for a while in the college, but they needed work, and the presiding pastor of Basel, Oswald Mykonius, wrote to Bucer. An invitation came from Strasbourg, and on October 17, 1542, the four exiles left Basel. Vermigli reported to his fellow believers in Lucca:

> With thankful hearts we traveled from Basel to Strasbourg. Immediately on our arrival we were received most cordially into Bucer's home. I was allowed to stay with him seventeen days. During this time, I saw in his preaching and conduct wonderful evidences of evangelical faith. He is so hospitable toward foreigners, who, for the sake of Christ and the Gospel, have had to travel to foreign places that his house resembles an inn.
>
> So well does he manage his family that during the whole time I spent with him I never noticed any trouble; rather, only what makes for edification. His table is neither splendid nor common, but ruled by a pious frugality. He makes no distinction regarding food for particular days. He enjoys everything, thanking God through Christ for his many and great gifts. Before and after the meal a passage from the Holy Scriptures is read. This then provides occasion for godly conversation. I can honestly say that

---

educated in the Augustinian Order, which he joined. He became influenced by the writing of Zwingli and Bucer, and, falling under suspicion by Rome, fled to Italy, taking refuge in Zurich, Basel, and, finally, Strasbourg. Here, with Bucer's help, he was appointed Professor of Theology and married a nun. Invited to England by Thomas Cranmer in 1547, he became Professor of Theology at Oxford. After the death of his wife in 1553, he was temporarily imprisoned by the Catholic Mary Tudor. Upon his release, he returned to Strasbourg as Professor and then to Zurich as Professor.

I always went away from this table more instructed, because every time I heard something I had earlier been unclear about or had yet some doubt about.

As for his other activities, I saw him always busy, and not with his own personal affairs, but whenever he could help the next person. He preaches untiringly, then again takes up the administration of the church, keeps watch that pastors direct the souls entrusted to them to the word of God, and leads the way by godly example. Further, he visits the schools so that the pains he has taken for them might result in the spread of the Gospel and the good of the children. Finally, he encourages and kindles the authorities to a Christian way of thinking and acting; almost no day goes by but that he visits the Town Hall. After he has spent the day in such labor, he dedicates the nights to study and prayer; never have I awakened from sleep without finding him awake. At one time he prepares himself for the sermon or lecture of the day; at another he pleads in prayer for power for the day's tasks.

That is the truly holy life, dear brethren, for the spiritual leaders of our time in the world, and all the more so in Christ's church.

Only a few weeks after Vermigli's arrival, Bucer received a commission that took him away from his church and family for almost a year. The Archbishop of Cologne, Hermann von Wied, was evangelically inclined and intended to implement the Reformation in his own spiritual domain. Accordingly, he summoned Bucer and Melanchthon[2] to his residence in Bonn.

---

2. Philip Melanchthon (1497–1560) was a humanist scholar and theologian who became aligned with Luther's Reformation teaching. In Wittenberg, he assisted Luther in the articulation of this teaching. He was

Initially, the work progressed with promise. On March 28, 1543, Bucer reported to his wife:

> You should boldly pray to God for our aged and pious Bishop and the work of the Lord that he pushes forward in a manly and determined manner. Today, God has granted a great grace; today, the Bishop has again become truly Bishop, and *Christian* Bishop. All counts, noblemen, and cities have pledged to him to inaugurate a Christian reformation and to advance it according to their means.

In fact, however, due to political events in the Empire, the Reformation work in Cologne came to a breakdown: Bucer had to return home without achieving his purpose, and Hermann von Wied was deposed.

During Bucer's absence, his wife gave birth to a son. He was named "Martin," after his father. In 1545, the girl, Elizabeth, followed. Moreover, Wibrandis adopted into her household, and, as her own child, little Margarethe Rosenblatt, youngest daughter of her deceased brother, Adelberg, the mintmaster in Colmar. In addition to these burdens came sorrows and troubles. We hear occasionally of the illness of the mother, Magdalena Strub, and of two daughters. The little boy just mentioned appears to have died an early death.

But, even more troubles were to follow.

---

an able Bible translator and commentator, and was a central figure at the Parliament of Augsburg (1530) that produced the Augsburg Confession.

6

Years of Exile: England

IN 1546, the tension in the Empire, due to the Reformation, exploded into a religious war. Strasbourg, too, participated in the struggle against the Emperor. But the evangelicals were beaten, the southern Germans already in 1546, and the Hessians and Saxons in 1547. The conditions imposed on the defeated were heavy: High reparation must be paid; above all, the Augsburg Parliament of May 1548 enacted a law whereby the Protestants should, in doctrine and ceremonies, return to the Catholic position, pending the final decision of the Adjudication Council then in progress; only the taking of the Lord's Supper in both kinds[1] and the marriage of wedded pastors would be allowed to continue in the meantime. Bucer, as one of the leading theologians of Protestantism, was ordered to Augsburg to endorse this law, but, instead, he there spurned this unreasonable demand with the greatest resolve, and fearing for his life he fled secretly from Augsburg.

In Strasbourg, too, Bucer fought to the utmost against the acceptance of the *Augsburger Interim* (as the law was called) in sermons and in petitions to the Council. Its acceptance would be nothing less than apostasy from Christ. But the Strasbourg Council was bound to the bidding of the Emperor and, therefore, had to agree that, at least in some of the Strasbourg churches, Catholicism could again be introduced. Further, it had to fulfill the demand of the imperial and episcopal councilors

---

1. That is, the reception of both the Eucharistic bread and wine by the laity, in contrast to the Catholic practice in which only the bread is received by the laity.

Woodcut depicting the hardships of family life in sixteenth-century Europe, including infant mortality

that it dismiss and deport the chief opponents of the *Interim*, namely, the pastors, Martin Bucer and Paul Fagius.[2] The Mayor of Strasbourg, Jakob Sturm, personally delivered to Bucer, his old friend and comrade in arms, the bitter announcement of his dismissal and expulsion.

Earlier, both of the Strasbourg theologians had been invited by Thomas Cranmer,[3] Archbishop of Canterbury, to come to England in order to help with the Reformation of the English church, which was aggressively pursued under the new King, Edward VI. This invitation they now accepted. On April 6, 1549, they left their beloved Strasbourg and made for England by way of Calais. During the summer, they were to devote themselves to theological work in the environment of the Archbishop, in Lambeth and Croyden, and, from the fall onward, to hold lectures at Cambridge University. Because of these events, the Bucer family was pressed to the limit.

Already in January 1548, in view of the gravity of the times, Bucer had drawn up a will that reflected his most important concerns. In the forefront, he placed loyalty to the severely threatened evangelical faith, to wit,

2. Paul Fagius (1504–49) was first a school teacher who became expert in Hebrew. In 1542, he went to Constance to work for the strengthening of the church there, and, in 1544, to Strasbourg as professor and preacher. With Bucer he was forced to flee Strasbourg to Cambridge where, for the short time preceding his death, he was Professor of Hebrew. His writings were dedicated almost exclusively to Hebrew philology and Old Testament interpretation.

3. Thomas Cranmer (1489–1556) was educated at Cambridge and ordained in 1523. In 1532, he was appointed Archbishop of Canterbury, became a principal tool in Henry VIII's overthrow of papal supremacy in England, and in Henry's divorces and marriages. During the reign of Mary Tudor, Cranmer temporarily pledged allegiance to Rome but recanted and was burned at the stake. His chief legacy lies with his contributions to Anglican worship, most notably the *Book of Common Prayer*.

> That my dear faithful wife, Wibrandis Rosenblatt, and our dear children of both parents, may continue with all diligence, and persist to the end in the faith and teaching that they heard from our dear, faithful fathers, Johannes Oecolampadius and Wolfgang Capito, as also from me.

Then follow directions concerning practical matters: Because Wibrandis had served him and his children so faithfully and, no doubt, will continue to do so, the allotment set for her widowhood should be increased by one-hundred florins; also, the interest she had brought to him from Basel should remain hers; fifty florins should "be set aside to our Lord Christ" for the poor and students; further, directions for Bucer's own children are addressed—Nathaniel, son of the first marriage, and the little daughter, Elizabeth, from the marriage with Wibrandis; finally, the stepchildren are not forgotten:

> . . . and because my daughters, Aletheia [Oecolampadius] and Agnes [Capito], have until now received no compensation for innumerable tasks and troubles which they had in my home, I determine that each receive ten florins from the share of my own children; but to each of the other two, Johann Simon [Capito] and Irene [Capito], a suit of clothes is to be given.

It was a great comfort for Bucer that, in the midst of the struggles over the introduction of the *Interim* in Strasbourg, his family received an additional masculine support owing to the fact that young Aletheia Oecolampadius married Bucer's trusted assistant, Pastor Christoph Söll of the Tyrol. On September 20, 1548, Bucer himself writes about it to Oswald Mykonius in Basel:

> Yesterday, I handed over Oecolampadius' and my daughter, Aletheia, in solemn marriage to Christoph Söll, a young man with burning love for Christ and for me. I couldn't have joined her to a more pious and true man. You're astonished, perhaps, at the boldness of this step in times so dangerous as these. But I couldn't leave my family (which, with the mother-in-law, numbers seven members) to any other protector who would be so faithful and in everything of a like mind with us. Next to Fagius, there's no one here who proclaims Christ's Kingdom so fervently and, at the same time, so popularly.

Not long after the wedding, Christoph Söll received Strasbourg citizenship through his connection with Aletheia.

When the painful separation had come, and Bucer went into exile in England, just before the crossing from Calais he wrote to his mentally and physically infirm son a fine letter of fatherly counsel:

> No little weed is so small but that it has its good effect. How much more, then, should man, created in the image of God, everywhere and always practice his useful effect: the honor of God and benefit towards neighbor. . . . I know well, unfortunately, your weakness in body and mind and have a truly fatherly compassion for you. Nevertheless, the Lord has given you your measure of his grace that you may learn and accomplish something. . . . You have a faithful guardian and also master. Esteem them in the Lord and honor the two ladies of the house as you would your own mother. Know also that my dear wife is so faithful to you that she really wants to be not a stepmother to you, but a genuine mother, and to show you every maternal loyalty.

> Listen to all these for your own good. Should the
> Lord grant that somehow I am again employed and
> can have you with me, you will see and know that
> I recognize and love you as my son, the only one
> from my dear deceased wife.

Although both theologians were received by Archbishop Cranmer in a very friendly manner, they felt, nonetheless, ill at ease in their new environment. In many ways the courtly life was especially troublesome for them. Fagius wrote to his wife: "We would prefer a bowl of onion soup and to be left in peace with one another." Therefore, they gladly seized Cranmer's suggestion that their families be allowed to follow (all the more because Bucer was suffering from colic and kidney stone) and wrote to Strasbourg with this intention. And, in fact, both families began preparations for the journey. Even Christoph Söll and his wife, Aletheia, wanted to come.

From the Lambeth Palace, Bucer replied in a fine letter of July 31, 1549, to Christoph Söll: His coming would be to Bucer a great boon, but it would burden his soul because Söll would, as a result, be withdrawn from the service of the Word in Strasbourg: "Let us not sin against Christ and the Church." Greetings and instructions were included for the other children: Aletheia [Oecolampadius] should be thoroughly compliant to her husband, he would lead her to God; they should pray for Bucer, their coming would be wonderful; but we are the Lord's and must serve him; Johann Simon [Capito] should study diligently and be obedient to his brother-in-law Christoph and his sister Aletheia.

> To you, dear son Nathaniel [Bucer], may God grant
> that you may fulfill what you promise. . . . Dear
> Agnes [Capito] I'm glad for your constant love
> for your mother and me. If you come, you must

> in any case bring a maid with you. And you, dear children, Margaretha [Rosenblatt], Irene [Capito], Lisbet [Bucer], may the Lord be with you. Hold the grandmother [Magdalena Strub] in honor and be obedient to her in all things. Study your catechism diligently.

A similar letter soon went off to his "beloved, pious, faithful" Wibrandis: In England, he is entirely unaccustomed to the cuisine—always meat and more meat, never, or seldom, any eggs, cabbage, or vegetables; he was especially concerned about the winter and his infirmities; if it should please God that she come, she should bring along Agnes Capito and the maid, Anna; God forbade him to let Christoph come, too, he is needed in the church as long as he can continue working in Strasbourg; if one hurries, one can be in England in eight days; it would be best for them to leave secretly from Strasbourg when the people are at Mass, and travel by means of a skiff as far as Oppenheim; there they would find ships to Mainz everyday; they should not travel without a man; but Christoph is not allowed to be this escort because he, Bucer, would be alarmed if Söll were to miss even one sermon; "preach, preach, whoever has a pulpit, as long as the Lord grants it." Then follow instructions that the mother, Magdalena Strub, be well cared for:

> May God help and comfort her in her old age, she who has known so much tribulation. She suits me very well. I would have gladly shared you with her, and, in fact, I would gladly leave you with her entirely . . . if I knew that God would rather have you with her than with me. God counsel and help us.

Then came short, warm messages to the rest of the family members: to Christoph Söll, Magdalena Strub, Aletheia Oecolampadius, Agnes, Johann Simon, and Irene Capito.

Finally, Bucer once again gives advice for the trip: In Antwerp, Frau Wibrandis should purchase spices, sugar, good plums, and such, because in England everything is so expensive; she should also bring medicine from Dr. Ulrich Geiger in Strasbourg because, again, in England the price is prohibitive; they should send the barrels[4] along with the baggage to London, but write the address exactly as he has given it. "The love of God be with you all. Amen."

The journey, indeed, took place. From the family of Paul Fagius went his wife and little daughter; from Bucer's family went Frau Wibrandis, Agnes Capito, perhaps also the little Elizabeth Bucer, and Anna the maid. We don't know who the male escort was.

Nothing is known about the reunion with the men, nor the beginning in Cambridge. That Paul Fagius died in Cambridge on November 13, 1549, is clearly established, and that in the spring of 1550 the women returned to Strasbourg company of Mathäus Nägelin, who had fled with Bucer and Fagius to England. The widow of Fagius remained there, and Wibrandis collected other family members to England. Only Agnes Capito was left behind with Bucer.

Soon after her arrival in Strasbourg, on June 25, 1550, Frau Wibrandis wrote the following letter to her husband:

> Grace and consolation from God, through our Lord Jesus Christ.
>
> Dear Father, today I traveled to Baden, to the spa, with Dr. Ulrich's wife, Mrs. Meier, Miss Elsbet, and Mr. George Münch's wife. I hope to bathe![5] I have good companionship, praise God.

4. At that time, a standard means of transporting household goods.

5. In the therapeutic mineral waters of Baden (= "Baths"), present day Baden-baden.

What I must write about, however, is something else. When I came back to Strasbourg, everyone was saying that you also had returned. Then the Papists got together and held a council as they wanted to scare you, and have let it out that they want to confiscate my property. Many have come to warn me. But I haven't burdened myself with the matter and have replied: Let them come. I'm not afraid of them. In the meantime, I've packed two barrels tight with belongings and delivered them to Mr. Burcher who shipped them off as soon as he could. This time I wasn't able to comply with our agreement that I should take everything myself. The situation was such that I didn't want to tempt fate, and for that reason I have shipped ahead the two barrels. Now I want to see how things go.

Something else happened. On the day before St. John's Day, someone named Velsius summoned me to appear next Thursday before the ecclesiastical court. The messenger announced the summons to Christoph [Söll] who answered that we will not appear, we are citizens, and if Velsius has a claim against us, well, there is a good public court here. So, he sent him back. He didn't tell me about it until he was already gone because he was worried that I might let fly some angry words, as, in fact, I might have! I've traveled to Baden and have directed Christoph [Söll] that he shouldn't answer them until I return. In the meantime, my barrels are sent off. Mr. Kniebis has counseled me that I shouldn't worry. So I haven't. I leave it to God. He will help me. Keep your chin up!

I and all our servants are well, and each sends greetings. Each of my bath-travelers sends greetings, too. God be with you. Greetings to Agnes [Capito], Niklaus [our colleague], and all our servants.

Written at the spa on the day after St. John's Day.

Your faithful wife,

Wibrandis Bucer

P.S. I have permitted two hundred Florins, deposited at St. Thomas', to be given to Mr. Burcher though Mr. Dasypodius.

While Wibrandis, along with her family, was preparing in Strasbourg for a new journey to England, Bucer, in England, was preparing for her arrival. Not only was the diet in England difficult for him, but also the English way of heating the rooms in winter.[6] What he needed were genuine German room stoves. The King had donated twenty pounds for the stove in his study, but that would be no help to his family. So, he dug deep into his pocket in order to make the house congenial for his relations.

In late summer, they began the journey: Frau Wibrandis, the aged mother Magdalena Strub, the children Elizabeth Bucer and Margaretha Rosenblatt, and as the male escort, this time none other than Christoph Söll. Frau Wibrandis brought letters from Strasbourg scholars to English scholars, and a couple of furs as a gift for the Archbishop of Canterbury.

About the family's stay in Cambridge, it is known only that already on October 14, 1550, Christoph Söll had returned so that he would miss as little as possible the preaching in Strasbourg, a town that was threatened by Catholicism. He took with him important writings of the Reformer addressing both the evangelical pastors of Strasbourg generally, and the Pastors Hedio, Hubert, and Beat Gerung in particular.

6. I.e., fireplaces, too drafty for Germans.

In the middle of February, 1551, Bucer again fell gravely ill. He composed an addendum to his Strasbourg will. He suggested to the executors that they remember how intensely Wibrandis gave of herself in the service of the church, first by the earnest and indefatigable work of Oecolampadius, then in the early years to the chronically ill Capito, and how she was burdened with the care of many guests, and also with illnesses right and left. Further directives concerned his various children, the niece Margaretha Rosenblatt, and the servants Margarethe and Martin; Agnes Capito was remembered with special warmth because she stayed behind with him in Cambridge when Frau Wibrandis returned home to fetch the wider family. Finally, the executors of the will were designated in Cambridge and Strasbourg: in Cambridge, two professors, the theologian Mathew Parker (later, Archbishop of Canterbury) and the lawyer Walter Haddon.

In the night of February 28 / March 1, 1551, Bucer died. The University of Cambridge prepared for him a solemn funeral. A long, warm letter of condolence was written to Frau Wibrandis by her former guest, Peter Martyr Vermigli, who was now a professor at Oxford, and Matthew Parker arranged a gift from the King, a widow's pension of a hundred English marks.

In April, the orphaned family set out on its journey home. Before the crossing, Frau Wibrandis reported from Gravesend to the executors in Cambridge about all sorts of financial matters: She had given her money, for the most part, to a businessman in London to be remitted in Strasbourg;[7] for the journey itself she had only ten pounds; if that isn't enough she would get more in Antwerp; the Archbishop of Canterbury had given her only forty pounds for the books (he said the Duchess of Suffolk had

---

7. I.e., by means of a letter of credit.

taken the best); "God be with you . . . my mother and my children greet you. Your servant in the Lord, Wibrandis."

Without incident, the party arrived in Strasbourg.

7

A Widow in Strasbourg and Basel

THE HEAVY burden of the *Augsburger Interim* continued to press on the evangelical churches of Germany. In Strasbourg, the Catholic service was held in the Cathedral, at New and Old St. Peter's, and in All Saints'. One anxiously waited for the final decision of the Council.

Just now, after a long interruption, the Council of Trent was reopened.[1] The Emperor requested the subordinated Protestants to send delegates in order, finally, to unite with the Catholic Church. In spite of serious objections, Strasbourg decided to comply with the will of the Emperor. The theologians, Johann Marbach and Christoph Söll (the husband of Aletheia), were designated as delegates. On February 29, 1552, they set out from Strasbourg, rendezvoused in Tübingen with theologians of the Duchy of Württemberg, and arrived at Trent on March 18.

In Strasbourg, one noted the activity of the two theologians with great interest. How demanding their mission was! They must not betray the truth of the Gospel.

Out of this concern, the young Aletheia Oecolampadius, who was not yet twenty-one, wrote the following letter to her husband:

---

1. The Council of Trent (Italy), which was held off and on over the years 1545–63, was motivated by the urgency of the Roman Catholic Church in counteracting the spread of Protestantism and effecting internal reforms.

To my kind, dear master Christoph Söll:

May grace, strength, and comfort in body and soul be bestowed upon us by God the Father, through his dear Son, our only Lord and Savior Jesus Christ, by the power of God the Holy Spirit. Amen.

O, my master, I have carefully read your letters. I'm very gratified that you have arrived in such good order. I'm always concerned that things won't go well for you, though I know that God is able to protect and shield you against violence and all evil. He alone, the good God, is powerful and mighty to preserve for his praise all those who trust in him. I know that you have held fast to this rock, Christ, and that you don't fear the world's power, as you shouldn't. What honors the Lord Jesus Christ, this you should promote and not fear. When someone asks you for counsel, you should counsel directly from the Word of God and subscribe to nothing else: God grant them according to their deeds. If we're innocent, it's enough. Don't compromise my Lord Christ; he can sustain you. Don't be afraid! Although I know you are of the same mind, I want you to know what is in my heart so that you can better carry on.

My soul is yours, whether in life or death as it pleases God. God grant faith and strength. Amen.

Then follows news about Strasbourg and personal matters: All three (that is, Aletheia, the maid, and the little child) have taken ill, so the mother, Frau Wibrandis, has brought them into her house and they are still with her.

I have yet much to write, but you know what sort of letter writer I am. Therefore this will have to do. No more at this time. God be with you. The mother [Frau Wibrandis] greets you, as does the grandmother [Magdalena Strub], Agnes [Capito], Margaretha [Rosenblatt], Irene [Capito], and Elisabeth [Bucer]. And give our friendly greetings to dear Doctor Marbach and to all pious brothers.

April 16

Your wife,

Alithie Söllin[2]

In Trent, the Strasbourg and Württemburg theologians soon recognized that they would not be admitted to any serious discussion at all, and on April 8, they had already left town, even before Aletheia's letter had been written. Also, the political reversal was now under way in which Prince Moritz of Saxon rose against the Emperor and nearly captured him in Innsbruck. The Council was adjourned and Protestantism was saved and was able, in time, to develop new life.

In the midst of all this, a new epidemic plague struck the region of the upper Rhine. In Basel, the famous Hebraist, Sebastian Münster, and the presiding Pastor, Oswald Mykonius, were carried off among the approximately one-thousand victims, and, in Strasbourg, Kaspar Hedio, and in May 1553, Christoph Söll. The young Aletheia was already a widow, and Frau Wibrandis lost in him a pillar of strength.

She resolved to return to Basel in the hope of maintaining her family more cheaply and more safely. On July 15, 1553, she reported this to her supporters in Cambridge, and, in fact, the move took place. Besides Frau Wibrandis, the move involved her mother, Magdalena Strub, and the children, Agnes Capito, Johann Simon Capito, Irene Capito, Elizabeth Bucer, as well as

2. "Alithie" is a nickname for "Aletheia"; "Söllin" is the feminine form of "Söll."

the niece, Margaretha Rosenblatt. Aletheia Oecolampadius, on the other hand, stayed in Strasbourg and married the pewtersmith, Hans von Lampertheim.

In Basel, Frau Wibrandis experienced joy and sorrow.

On September 5, 1555, her daughter, Agnes Capito, married Jakob Meyer, the grandson of Jakob Meyer of Hirzen, the Mayor of Basel with whom we are well acquainted. Jakob Meyer was, at that time, Pastor in Arlesheim. One year later, when Margrave Karl II of Baden-Durlach implemented the Reformation in his territory, he was Pastor in Petersberg near Sulzberg, and, in 1560, he accepted a call to be Pastor at Muttenz.[3] During these years, his wife Agnes presented him with several children, though a few died at tender ages.

Frau Wibrandis' son, Johann Simon Capito, caused her a lot of grief. Soon after the move to Basel, we encounter him as a theology student at the University, and, in 1556, he went to Marburg to continue his studies. Nothing good came of it. In March 1557, Frau Wibrandis wrote him a forceful letter. On the envelope she wrote:

> To
> The honorable and learned
> Johann Simon Capito
> Student at Marburg

But in the letter itself she enjoined:

> Grace and comfort and much wisdom and knowledge from God through our Lord Jesus Christ.
>
> Dear Hans Simon, I've had no further word from you since the messenger from Marburg was here. But I know well that, if I had, it wouldn't

---

3. Arlesheim, a village a few miles south of Basel; Muttenz, a village a few miles up the Rhine from Basel.

> have pleased me because it's just like you to give me nothing but trouble. If only I should live long enough to hear something good from you! Then I would I die happy.

His fellow students are already pastors in the Margrave's territory. He certainly knows what his dear father dedicated him to: "Live up to it! You are no longer a child." He should be thrifty and study hard, not drink, not gamble, and shun evil company; he should flee the evil world and become a servant of Christ as his dear father was. This would give her great joy, and also the grandmother, the sisters, the brothers-in-law, and all the friends.

> There is none among us who wouldn't lay down life and limb for you if only you'd pull yourself together a little. Otherwise, we'll let you squander what you have, and when you have no more you'll have to look elsewhere because then there'll be no one to give you a cent. So, straighten up!

Agnes is with her husband in the Margrave's territory and all's well with them; the Margrave has endowed scholarships for twelve students; if he, Hans Simon, would come to Basel and do the right thing she would obtain one for him.

> If you want to do the right thing, then come home. If not, then do what you want. But I advise you to be thrifty with what you have. I wish you a good year.
>
> Your faithful mother,
>
> Wibrandis

This letter is the last we hear of Frau Wibrandis.

In 1564, the region of the upper Rhine was visited by a new plague epidemic. In Strasbourg, 5,000 would die and in Basel 7,000.[4] Christian Wurstisen reported that the Basel death toll was heaviest in August.

> ... everyday, such a multitude of men, women, and children died off that each one could no longer be buried individually; great pits were dug and a dozen or two buried together. It is unbelievable how, from about midday until about 2:00 and 4:00 o'clock in the afternoon, the bodies were carried from all the streets to the pits in the attempt to get the dead buried.

On November 1, 1564, Frau Wibrandis also fell victim to this plague epidemic. But she was not buried in a mass grave; she was interred in the grave of her husband, Oecolampadius, in the cloisters of the Münster.

Soon thereafter, Paul Cherler, a theology student in Basel and then Pastor in Binzen in the Margrave's territory, published a collection of little poems on some of the victims Great Death. Two of the poems are dedicated to Frau Wibrandis Rosenblatt. In the first, we find the lines:

> Lovely was this rose,
> not a more beautiful borne
> by Switzerland fields,
> or the soil of Alsace.

---

4. The modern estimate is that there were about 4,000 Basel deaths due to this plague—still, a significant number in a city of 12,000 people.

8

Children and Grandchildren

THE CHILDREN and grandchildren, many of whom owed much to the remarkable woman who had been their mother and grandmother, lived long.

Of the daughter from the first marriage, Wibrandis Keller, we hear that in 1541 she married the Strasbourger, Hans Jeliger. She appears to have been widowed early and then to have married Jakob Gysin. In any case, a Wibrandis Keller died in 1582 in Sissach, in the region of Basel, wife of this man and mother of a flourishing family.

It's not known whether Aletheia Oecolampadius passed on the family of her father (the Basel Reformer and her mother, Wibrandis) through her first marriage to Christoph Söll or her second to Hans von Lampertheim.

On the other hand, the descendants from Agnes Capito are numerous. In fact, during her mother's lifetime she had presented her husband with seven children, and when, in 1565, Jakob Meyer came as Pastor to St. Alban's in Basel, seven more children were born to them. The first girl born after the grandmother's death received her name, "Wibrandis." The youngest child, the son, Wolfgang, became an important theologian. In his youth, he was able to study for some time in Cambridge by means of a scholarship he received in honor of his late step-grandfather, Martin Bucer. When he died, in 1653, he was interred in the grave of Oecolampadius and his grandmother, Wibrandis, in the cloisters of the Basel Cathedral.

The end of Hans Simon Capito is a sad one. The mother's letter and other scolding availed nothing. In 1567, he was declared missing, and Aletheia Oecolampadius, the wife of Hans von Lampertheim, was appointed beneficiary, no doubt because she and Christoph Söll had taken special care of him while the mother was in England.

Irene Capito was married a second time, in the late 1560's, to Johann Lukas Iselin.[1] She also honored her mother by bestowing her name on one of her children: A little boy received the name "Wibrandus," a dignified name related in form to the better known names "Hildebrandus" and "Hadubrandus."

The youngest daughter, Elizabeth Bucer, married the Basel Councilman, Karl Gleser, in 1565. At the side of her husband she was, for a time, governess of Waldenburg.[2] The marriage produced twelve or thirteen children. The first daughter was named "Wibrandis." The son, Adelberg, appears to have taken somewhat after his step-uncle, Hans Simon Capito. In any case, against his widowed mother's will, he ran away to England where, nonetheless, at Cambridge a scholarship was awarded to him, as well as to his cousin, Wolfgang Meyer, in memory of his grandfather, Bucer. Once, he received a stern letter from his mother. She implored him to invest his youth well and not to let an hour slip by that was wasted, for there is no greater loss than when youth invest their time badly, because this, unlike money or property, may never be retrieved. As concerns his name, he should keep his father's name—he had been a religious and honorable man that Adelberg shouldn't be ashamed of; but if he wants to change it, he should sign himself "Gleser, surnamed Bucer," without any bigger change. The letter concludes:

---

1. The Iselin family is an example of Basel families of importance since the Reformation. The Staehelins were also such.

2. A village southeast from Basel, about 20 minutes by train.

> Now God be with you and protect you. May he send you an angel to lead and guide you on all blessed paths!

Through all these children and grandchildren, Frau Wibrandis is the ancestress of many descendants living yet today in the city and region of Basel. May these descendants, together with all other members of our Christian community, allow themselves, through God's Holy Spirit, to be instruments of the Church of Christ. Frau Wibrandis was such an instrument, in all human weakness and in the power of God.

Picture Credits

Blarer / *Contemporary Portraits of Reformers of Religion and Letters* (London: Religious Tract Society, 1906).

Bucer / *Martin Bucer and Sixteenth Century Europe*, ed. Christian Krieger and Marc Lienhard (Leiden: Brill, 1993), vol. 1, p. 18.

Capito / *Martin Bucer and Sixteenth Century Europe*, ed. Christian Krieger and Marc Lienhard (Leiden: Brill, 1993), vol. 2, p. 472.

Dance of Death / Roland H. Bainton, *Women of the Reformation in Germany and Italy* (Minneapolis: Augsburg, 1971), p. 78.

Erasmus / A. G. Dickens and Whitney R. D. Jones, *Erasmus the Reformer* (London: Mandarin, 1994), p. 179.

Oecolampadius / Roland H. Bainton, *Women of the Reformation in Germany and Italy* (Minneapolis: Augsburg, 1971), p. 83.

Signatories / *Martin Bucer and Sixteenth Century Europe*, ed. Christian Krieger and Marc Lienhard (Leiden: Brill, 1993), vol. 1, p. 418.

St. Thomas / Roland H. Bainton, *Women of the Reformation in Germany and Italy* (Minneapolis: Augsburg, 1971), p. 58.

Wibrandis / Roland H. Bainton, *Women of the Reformation in Germany and Italy* (Minneapolis: Augsburg, 1971), p. 80.

Zwingli / Paul A. Russell, *Lay Theology in the Reformation: Popular Pamphleteers in Southwest Germany 1521–1525* (Cambridge: Cambridge University Press, 1986), p. 66.

Bibliographical Note

IN ADDITION to the present little book, treatments of Wibrandis include the following biographical essays: Otto Michaelis, "Wibrandis Rosenblatt," in *Elässiche Gestalten* (Strasbourg: Evangelische Buchhandlung, 1942); Maria Heinsius, "Wibrandis Rosenblatt," in *Das Unüberwindliche Wort* (Munich: Kaiser, 1951); Roland Bainton, "Wibrandis Rosenblatt," in *Women of the Reformation in Germany and Italy* (Minneapolis: Augsburg Press, 1971), appearing initially in the *Festschrift* for Ernst Staehelin on his eightieth birthday, *Gottesreich und Menschenrecht*, ed. Max Geiger (Basel: Helbing & Lichtenhahn, 1969). For a brief sketch, see René Teuteberg, "Wibrandis Rosenblatt," in *Der Reformation verpflichtet: Gestalten und Gestalter in Stadt und Landschaft Basel aus fünf Jahrhunderten*, ed. Rudolf Suter and René Teuteberg (Basel: Christoph-Merian, 1979); and for a brief notice see *Basler Heimatsgeschichte: Heimatgeschichtliches Lesebuch von Basel*, ed. Fritz Meier, fifth ed. (Basel: Lehrmittelverlag des Kanton Basel-Stadt, 1974), pp. 622–23, which describes her as a "feinfühlige, tapfere und opfermutige Frau" ("sensitive, brave, and self-sacrificing woman"). But the above treatments are largely dependent on Staehelin's *Frau Wibrandis* itself.

In-depth research into the life of Wibrandis, the various players in her drama, the circumstances of her years, etc., would require attention to material in the city archives and university libraries of Basel and Strasbourg. This would include Stahelin's two-volume *Briefe und Akten zum Leben Oekolampads* (Leipzig: Hensius Nachfolger, 1927–34) which provides documentation for many episodes in Wibrandis' life. More general, and more accessible, are the relevant entries as in *Allgemeine deutsche Biographie* (Berlin: Dunker & Humbolt, reprint 1970); *The*

Oxford Dictionary of the Christian Church, ed. F. L. Cross and E. A. Livingstone, second ed. (Oxford, England: Oxford University Press, 1974); *Encyclopedic Dictionary of Religion*, ed. Paul Kevin Meagher, *et al.* (Washington, D.C.: Corpus Publications, 1979); the more extensive entries in the multivolume *Theologische Realenzyklopädie*, ed. Gerhard Krause and Gerhard Müller (Berlin: de Gruyter, 1977–); Staehelin provides no documentation in *Frau Wibrandis*, even of quoted material. There is, in fact, no single way of documenting the various letters, and one interested in this should consult the bibliographic direction given at the end of Bainton's article, cited above.

As was said in the Introduction, most of what we know about Wibrandis we know through accounts about her various husbands, thus works on them are important for Wibrandis study. Some of these are Ernst Staehelin, *Brief und Akten zum Leben Oekolampads* (already cited); J. W. Baum, *Capito and Butzer* (Nieuwkoop: de Graaf, 1967, orig. 1860); A. E. Harvey, *Martin Bucer in England* (Marburg: Bauer, 1906); Hastings Eels, *Martin Bucer* (New Haven, Conn.: Yale University Press, 1931); Constantin Hopf, *Martin Bucer and the English Reformation* (New York: Macmillan, 1947); J. M. Kittelson, *Wolfgang Capito: From Humanist to Reformer* (Leiden: Brill, 1969); Ed. L. Miller, "Oecolampadius: The Unsung Hero of the Basel Reformation," *The Iliff Review*, 39 (1982); Martin Greschat, *Martin Bucer: a Reformer and His Time*, tr. Stephen Buckwalter (Louiville: Westminster/John Knox, 2004).

On related topics: Miriam Usher Chrisman, *Strasbourg and the Reform: A Study in the Process of Change* (Haven: Yale University Press, 1967); Gordon Rupp, *Patterns of Reformation* (Philadelphia: Fortress Press, 1969), Part I; David C. Steinmetz, *Reformers in the Wings* (Grand Rapids, Mich.: Baker, 1971); Miriam U. Chrisman, "Women and the Reformation in Strasbourg," *Archiv für Reformationsgeschichte*, 63 (1972);

Steven E. Ozment, *The Reformation in the Cities: The Appeal of Protestantism to Sixteenth-Century Germany and Switzerland* (New Haven, Conn.: Yale University Press, 1975); Hans R. Guggisberg, *Basel in the Sixteenth Century: Aspects of the City before, during, and after the Reformation* (St. Louis: Center for Reformation Research, 1982); Heide Wunder, ed., *Eine Stadt der Frauen: Studien und Quellen zur Geschichte der Baslerinnen im späten Mittelalter und zu Beginn der Neuzeit (13.–17. Jh.)* (Basel: Helbing & Lichtenhahn, 1995); Susan C. Karant-Nunn, "Reformation Society, Women and the Family," in *The Reformation World*, ed. Andrew Pettegree (London: Routledge, 2000).

www.ingramcontent.com/pod-product-compliance
Lightning Source LLC
Chambersburg PA
CBHW051707090426
42736CB00013B/2584